BE CAUSE!

I HAVE ALL THAT I DESIRE

ZONUN DHAKA

Made with ♥ on the Notion Press Platform
www.notionpress.com

Contents

Contents

Preface

Take a deep breath and thank yourself for picking this book to be your next or first read if you are somebody who does not read at all. Sounds like a big statement but it is what it is. I want you to do this because YOU have written this book FOR YOURSELF.

I am just one of the eight billion people on this earth that had to move to put things into words and make this happen FOR YOU to read. It could happen because you desired to read it and have given me your words and I have only written what your consciousness wanted you to read at this very moment.

The fact that I could write it and you are reading it is in itself a testimony of what is written in it actually works.

We think of things we want and desire all day long but more than that we keep reminding ourselves of everything we do not want all through and beyond time; ignoring the fact that YOU are always listening to it, THE ONE who is going to bring them into your reality that you experience.

So, ever thought what you are telling yourself to do? Yes, you tell all your desires to kill themselves and then long over their dead bodies to manifest themselves taking the role of a victim.

When all you have ever done is constantly remind yourself of all that you do not want to manifest. That is what your consciousness believes to be true and abundance being the default nature of universe which means yourself too; gives you an abundance of all that you do not want.

Your state of being comes from an energy of lack and desperation. It comes from having a belief of wanting them in a moment that does not exist in the now. It comes from a fearful consciousness that tells you to put too much logic and distrust and a constant need to check back whether it is happening for you or not.

It leaves you in a constant state of worry and further deep into the state of lack until it becomes a loop and where you find yourself endlessly running and being a part of what they call a rat race.

This book is a reminder; a talk with your true nature/ supreme consciousness that is ready to give you all that you desire. Because it is creation itself.

It exists in THE NOW and it wants to tell you THE HOW of it as there are infinite ways of your manifestations to come to you. Because pondering on THE HOW AND THE WHEN is not the job of your ego mind as you may think it is and constantly fail even after using your logical reasoning and putting the so called endless efforts. Get up, sit on a comfortable floor and listen to what you have to say to yourself.

Acknowledgements

I WANT TO SINCERELY THANK ANYONE READING
THE BOOK BEACUSE
IT WAS YOUR DESIRE TO READ IT
THAT MADE ME WRITE IT

Prologue

HOW TO READ THE BOOK

- The book is written in a dialogue manner where you (represented as ME) and true self (represented as I AM) are having a conversation.

- It has been divided into twelve chapters but still to be read in a continuous manner as the chapters do not represent any separate concept or technique (because there are none) that are discrete or disconnected to each other.

- These chapters have been provided for convenience for a later read or a conversation that you might intend or desire to have with yourself over a certain portion depending upon where you are in your journey.

- The book can be used as a simple guide anytime and anywhere. You can open any page of the book and will get what you were looking for in that moment.

- Remember throughout and after reading that it is a conversation you had with yourself. Therefore, it's going to be different for you or somebody else doing it as we are unique individuals.

- The same dialogue or chapter is going to feel different every time you will pick up the book as it depends on who you are being when having this conversation at that moment.

- Chapter twelve is a two-page empty chapter for you (I AM) to write all that you are and your desires. Then simply be and watch them come to you as you are the creator.

• x •

Chapter 1 - THE RUN

RUNNING TOWARDS SOMETHING OR AWAY FROM IT

I

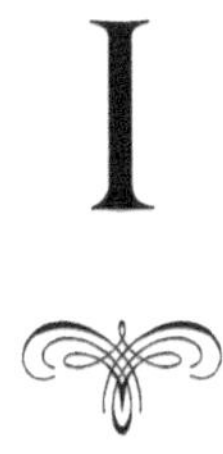

THE RUN

ME- *I am tired of running. Tired of this race that every single being on this earth is a part of. You know, we call it a rat race.*

Some of us think that we are ahead of others while some just have made peace with them being close to the starting line and for how long; even they have no idea.

Then there are those who do not want to be a part of it all but still somehow want to reach the finish line.

I AM - Hmmm...so where do you see yourself? Standing or should I ask "are you even standing if at all." Forget about the finish line; Do you even remember your starting point? Who decided it and when was the exact time you decided to run?

ME- I am in my early 20s and already working a high paying job so I believe I am ahead of a big lot. But when I look at my personal life I feel I have not got much out of it.

That confuses me and I believe maybe I am not that good of a runner after all. I cannot clearly see or define to you where or when did I start to run but I guess I AM RUNNING.

I AM- Then why do you feel tired when you are admitting that you feel you are ahead in the race?

Doesn't that make you feel good and run more and may be with greater speed?

ME- *To tell you the truth I sometimes feel I don't know what I am running for and that makes me quit the race once and for all.*

I AM- *So, did u ask yourself what are you running for?*

ME- *Now I have come to a point where I am only running just to avoid being run over and the start line has become hazy. Speaking of the finish line; they say nobody has seen it. All I can see for now is just people ahead of me and people behind me; people left to me and people right to me. It's a maze.*

I AM- *Hmm, avoid being run over, sounds practical!*

So are you trying to say these people are blocking your view of the finish line?

ME- *No, I guess I am going to and fro or may be its more than one race I am running.*

I AM- **take a deep breath and tell me, Is this race towards a goal or are you running away from something?**

ME – *Yes, I am actually trying to run away more than towards something. Its not one race. Infact, I have actually stepped in quite a few of them.*

Few enough to never make me finish any!

Will I be running like this forever and still not reach the finish line. May be I would not hate running this much if at all I knew the why.

I AM- *hmmm, Tell me more, don't hesitate. Afterall we are all the same. I AM YOU.*

ME- *I guess I want to say that I am are tired of running after my desires and making the best out of life but nothing actually seem to work out in my favour and now I am at a point where I am barely surviving.*

Chapter 2- THE LONGING vs THE ONLY TRUE MOMENT

IT CAME AND ITS COMING MADE ME GO BACK IN TIME JUST TO LONG FOR ITS ARRIVAL

II

THE LONGING *vs* THE ONLY TRUE MOMENT

I AM- *Let me be very blunt and clear with you. Bear with me.*

You are the killer of your own manifestations. They are always yours. They have always been yours. Because they exist right NOW. They exist in the PRESENT. That is why we say manifestation is instant.

You kill it by refusing to be in the moment. Yes, it's as simple as it sounds.

For your manifestations/desires to materialize; it needs a state of awareness or universe that actually exists and that which is the truth. That which is the ultimate reality.

PRESENT IS THE ONLY TRUTH, NEITHER PAST NOR FUTURE CAN OR DOES HAVE AN EXISTENCE.

The universe has existence as a supreme combined consciousness and all beings the parts of it; have some portion of it activated in various degrees or we can say we access it in a very limited sense to help this supreme consciousness experience its own nature in an elaborate way.

Our only way to get complete access to this supreme consciousness or the gateway to all our manifestations and desires is THE PRESENT MOMENT.

We divide this infinite consciousness into pieces using time viz past present and future in order to understand this universe and make sense of our lives and call it being practical while using only our limited sense organs and just the ego mind.

Therefore, the key to manifestation is realizing your true nature which is that of the infinite consciousness and it is here NOW in the present moment; available to you, because this is only where it can exist.

ME- *How do I be in the NOW or present? How do I let the universe or supreme consciousness know my intensions or desires?*

How would it ever know?

I AM- *Hmm, now you have asked me the right question.*

You are actually trying to run away from the present moment that existed just before and running towards a present moment that would exist just after this moment in future (that is what your rat race is all about)

Understand this- It came and its coming made me go back in time just to long for its arrival.

Yes, you do that knowingly/unknowingly, but it has the same effect.

When in reality the universe is right here right now offering you all of it. But you are busy running away from and running again only towards the longing of it. You are denying the existence of this present moment in which YOU, YOUR PHYSICAL BODY, YOUR PHYSICAL REALITY AND THEREFORE YOUR MANIFESTATION EXISTS.

Universe can only and only exist in the present moment and therefore all that you desire can only be manifested by you when you are there in the present moment and not somewhere in past or future.

Chapter 3- THE UNKNOWN

IS THE UNIVERSE TAKING YOU SOMEWHERE OR YOU ARE THE ONE LEADING?

III

THE UNKNOWN

ME- *But why would I do that? Why would I want to run away from it? Why would I run away from my own desires?*

I AM- "THE UNKNOWN"

When we operate from the limited consciousness and only the ego mind of ours using our limited sense organs. We create a fearful piece of consciousness which finds comfort only in the known (which it perceives to be the past; even the past as close as the last second that passed).

For this fearful consciousness to step into the present is not possible. Because stepping in the present would mean leaving behind the known reality and going into an unknown reality. This fearful consciousness perceives the unknown as a threat to its existence and therefore it resists any change.

It wants to stay in the same situation. To this fearful consciousness it does not matter whether its existing in its desired reality or not. It simply wants to exist. To it stepping into the unknown means the end of all. All that it had known and which appears to it as threat. It is simply its little way to keep itself alive.

A very simple example of which you see literally in your daily life (to put it practically) is where despite a student knowing he should be studying a day before exam but he simply keep himself busy with his phone and doesn't seem to put it dow

The fear of stepping into the future (the present moment just next to in what you are literally existing now) is even more. Here the uncertainty further increases because now it would depend on the choices and experience of the NOW / PRESENT.

It will completely change the trajectory of **where the universe is going to take you or rather where you going to take the universe.**

(Yes! knowingly or unknowingly, YOU DO. You take the universe wherever it is now).

ME- *How can I take the universe anywhere or how do I control it?*

By simply being in the PRESENT MOMENT or in your present case by running away from it. You are constantly interacting with it. You are listening to the voice of the universe where it is telling you its desires for you and itself and in turn YOU telling it softly what you desire to experience through it.

By merging your consciousness with the supreme consciousness and realising that your existence in 3D is possible only by the PRESNT MOMENT'S EXISTENCE.

*Hence, all your desires exist in **THE PRESENT MOMENT**. They are yours right now, right here in this moment; waiting for you to realise their existence and experience them.*

And this is your answer, you do not have to control universe or anything for that matter. You simply have to control your own ego mind and focus your attention in the present moment; the here and now!

About taking the universe anywhere, you simply use your consciousness to talk to the supreme consciousness and let your desires be known and make your choice as per your intended desire.

ME- How can I talk to the universal/ supreme consciousness and how do I even make a choice and let it be known? I cant even seem to be heard even by my pet (jokingly).

I AM- Hahaha! Listen,

In order to connect to the supreme consciousness/universe, go to the source of it "NOTHINGNESS."

In order to talk to the supreme consciousness/universe, use "SEILENCE."

In order to reach to the supreme consciousness/universe, go to the place "WHERE INSPIRATION COMES FROM."

ME- *This is whole another level stuff to me. Elaborate please, because although I do not undertand it but somehow it sounds promising.*

I AM- *Because it is.*

I will explain it to you in detail at the right time but before we go there you need to have more doubts and I can see you already have them.

ME- *Yes! definitely, I do have doubts and a lot of them. After all this I am left with a choice to make and I have to do it every moment. Are you implying that in the end I am going to decide what will happen next in the universe and let my decision be known to the universe for it to act on it?*

I AM-Exactly, it means that we are the creator of our own world and these are all our own choices that have guided the universe to be in the way it is presented to you or working for you.

It also implies that whatever situation we are in right now, is a result of our choices and

IT WAS YOU WHO TOLD THE UNIVERSE TO BE LIKE THIS FOR YOURSLEF (knowingly / unknowingly).

Because the universe is always looking at you even in the darkness, it is always listening to you even in the silence and always responding to you even when you are unaware of its presence.

Above all, it is always here IN THE PRESENT WAITING WITH ITS EAR TO YOUR HEART FOR YOU TO TELL IT YOUR DESIRES; YOUR CHOICE OF HOW YOU WANT TO EXPERINCE IT. It is always ready to show you its power and give you all you have ever desired and all the experiences you long for.

Tell it without doubt and tell it with clarity and experience them being given to you RIGHT HERE RIGHT NOW, IN THIS PRESENT MOMENT.

REMEMBER, MANIFESTATION IS INSTANT.

IT IS AND HAS ALWAYS BEEN HERE IN THE PRESENT MOMENT.

ME- *But why would I do that? Why would I want to run away from it? Why would I run away from my own desires?*

I AM- *"THE UNKNOWN"*

When we operate from the limited consciousness and only the ego mind of ours using our limited sense organs. We create a fearful piece of consciousness which finds comfort only in the known (which it perceives to be the past; even the past as close as the last second that passed).

For this fearful consciousness to step into the present is not possible. Because stepping in the present would mean leaving behind the known reality and going into an unknown reality. This fearful consciousness perceives the unknown as a threat to its existence and therefore it resists any change.

It wants to stay in the same situation. To this fearful consciousness it does not matter whether its existing in its desired reality or not. It simply wants to exist. To it stepping into the unknown means the end of all. All that it had known and which appears to it as threat. It is simply its little way to keep itself alive.

A very simple example of which you see literally in your daily life (to put it practically) is where despite a student knowing he should be studying a day before exam but he simply keep himself busy with his phone and doesn't seem to put it down.

The fear of stepping into the future (the present moment just next to in what you are literally existing now) is even more. Here the uncertainty further increases because now it would depend on the choices and experience of the NOW / PRESENT.

*It will completely change the trajectory of **where the universe is going to take you or rather where you going to take the universe.***

(Yes! knowingly or unknowingly, YOU DO. You take the universe wherever it is now).

ME- *How can I take the universe anywhere or how do I control it?*

By simply being in the PRESENT MOMENT or in your present case by running away from it. You are constantly interacting with it. You are listening to the voice of the universe where it is telling you its desires for you and itself and in turn YOU telling it softly what you desire to experience through it.

By merging your consciousness with the supreme consciousness and realising that your existence in 3D is possible only by the PRESNT MOMENT'S EXISTENCE.

Hence, all your desires exist in THE PRESENT MOMENT. They are yours right now, right here in this moment; waiting for you to realise their existence and experience them.

And this is your answer, you do not have to control universe or anything for that matter. You simply have to control your own ego mind and focus your attention in the present moment; the here and now!

About taking the universe anywhere, you simply use your consciousness to talk to the supreme consciousness and let your desires be known and make your choice as per your intended desire.

ME- *How can I talk to the universal/ supreme consciousness and how do I even make a choice and let it be known? I cant even seem to be heard even by my pet (jokingly).*

I AM- Hahaha! Listen,

*In order to connect to the supreme consciousness/universe, go to the source of it "**NOTHINGNESS.**"*

*In order to talk to the supreme consciousness/ universe, use "**SEILENCE.**"*

*In order to reach to the supreme consciousness/universe, go to the place "**WHERE INSPIRATION COMES FROM.**"*

ME- *This is whole another level stuff to me. Elaborate please, because although I do not undertand it but somehow it sounds promising.*

I AM- *Because it is.*

I will explain it to you in detail at the right time but before we go there you need to have more doubts and I can see you already have them.

ME- *Yes! definitely, I do have doubts and a lot of them. After all this I am left with a choice to make and I have to do it every moment. Are you implying that in the end I am going to decide what will happen next in the universe and let my decision be known to the universe for it to act on it?*

I AM-Exactly, it means that we are the creator of our own world and these are all our own choices that have guided the universe to be in the way it is presented to you or working for you.

It also implies that whatever situation we are in right now, is a result of our choices and

IT WAS YOU WHO TOLD THE UNIVERSE TO BE LIKE THIS FOR YOURSLEF (knowingly / unknowingly).

Because the universe is always looking at you even in the darkness, it is always listening to you even in the silence and always responding to you even when you are unaware of its presence.

Above all, it is always here IN THE PRESENT WAITING WITH ITS EAR TO YOUR HEART FOR YOU TO TELL IT YOUR DESIRES; YOUR CHOICE OF HOW YOU WANT TO EXPERINCE IT. It is always ready to show you its power and give you all you have ever desired and all the experiences you long for.

Tell it without doubt and tell it with clarity and experience them being given to you RIGHT HERE RIGHT NOW, IN THIS PRESENT MOMENT.

REMEMBER, MANIFESTATION IS INSTANT.

IT IS AND HAS ALWAYS BEEN HERE IN THE PRESENT MOMENT.

Chapter4- UNCERTAINITY

EXPECT THE UNEXPECTED

IV

UNCERTAINITY

ME- *So, tell me what is this unknown? Can I trust it? How would I know if I am even making the right choice?*

I AM- Uncertainty implies that anything is possible and nothing is impossible for this universe.

What the next moment is going to bring is unknown/uncertain and there is no way to know but to simply accept and experience it when it comes. Therefore, trust in the present moment, make the choice and simply tell the universe. Let it know and watch the magic begin and create the universe around you as YOU want to experience it.

And hence, overthinking/thinking, worrying, or having any doubts whatsoever in the next moment of universe is baseless and should be discarded to experience its magic and help it work for you.

You do not need to know THE HOW!?

Trust the universe and then watch the beauty unfold.

"EXPECT THE UNEXPECTED."

Chapter 5- THE VICTIM

COMFORT OF THE FAMILIARITY

V

THE VICTIM

I AM- *You need to understand that life (universe) always wants to work for you and not against you. It is working out perfectly. The universe understands your needs better than you. Your job is to continually surrender and trust the universe.*

It all comes down to your attitude towards it. You sabotage all your manifestations/ dreams/ desires by your lack of trust in the universe. By your attitude of distrust, you yourself tell the universe to not work in your favour.

When you choose distrust in universe it shows you an unfriendly face of itself. Because abundance is the default state of universe and hence yourself too. By expressing distrust you create an abundant cycle of distrust as universe simply fulfil your desires and commands. This is exactly the moment when you take the victim role.

ME- VICTIM ROLE? What does that supposed to mean here and why would I take this victim role anyway?

I AM- *Being in a state of distrust and staying triggered gives you a sense of comfort.*

The "COMFORT OF THE FAMILIARITY." Howsoever negative it may be , you get addicted to those negative attributes. Then universe simply obeys your commands. Here those are coming with a background of resentment, anger and all sorts of negativity and gives you a reality based on that.

Playing the victim in this situation satisfies your fearful ego mind (talked about ego in chapter two) and makes it feel as if it is not the problem and it had been wronged.

Remember that this fearful ego mind fears living in the present moment and defies the reality to feel comfortable. Hence takes you away from awareness. •

Chapter 6- SURRENDER

THE ACTUAL WAY TO TAKE CONTROL

VI

SURRENDER

ME- *How do I exactly get out of this victim role?*

I AM- *You can get away from it by simply creating more space. Through awareness you create more space. Then, you will be able to identify these patterns in you to be less reactive. You will be able to bring your awareness back to the default state which is the state of abundance.*

ME- *I am getting really impatient here. Straightway just tell me how do I actually create that space and What do you imply by being less reactive?*

I AM-Complete surrender and trusting the universe

SURRENDERING IS THE ACTUAL WAY TO TAKE CONTROL

When you stop trying to control every aspect of your life, your burden is going to be relieved and you will be able to catch up with the flow of universe/supreme consciousness and everything will take care of itself without you needing to be involved too much.

We spend our lives trying to get peace, joy, abundance but it was always ours the whole time, because that is the default state of being of the universal consciousness.

By surrendering to it, we continue to return to the present moment of beingness. RIGHT HERE, RIGHT NOW in the PRESENT MOMENT which the only REALITY.

the only space where our dreams and manifestations can and do exist. Then all the actions and results take care of themselves.

The deeper you go into the present moment, the more you can build the foundation of your life in the space, the more life becomes effortless.

You naturally allow the flow of life which is the source of all peace, joy and abundance and everything works out perfectly on its own without you needing to do very much of anything.

Chapter 7- THE DEEP DIVE

TALKING WITH THE SILENCE AND GOING TO THE PLACE WHERE INSPIRATION COMES FORM

VII

THE DEEP DIVE

ME- *By now I have understood that I need to surrender and keep reminding myself to come back to the present moment and be in the default state that is the state of abundance. How do I go deeper in the present moment and stay there? Going into the state is still easy but what is really the issue is to stay there for as long as one wants.*

I AM- *Here we come back to it.*

In order to connect to the supreme consciousness/ universe, go to the source of it **"NOTHINGNESS."**

In order to talk to the supreme consciousness/ universe, use **"SEILENCE."**

In order to reach to the supreme consciousness/ universe , go to the place " **WHERE INSPIRATION COMES FROM."**

ME- *We had talked about it earlier but not in detail, although now at this point I have at least got an idea of how to approach this coming thought. I am felling ready to receive it now. Tell me!*

I AM- *It is in silence, in stillness that our ego mind disappears. Silence and stillness, bring us to the present and in the present moment that fearful ego mind cannot exist.*

A simple technique is to sit still in solitude and simply watch your breath without trying to manipulate it.

There is a space (gap) between you taking in the breath and giving it back to the universe and again a space when you have given it back and you take it again from universe and THIS IS THE SPACE / THE LACK/ THE GAP / THIS DESIRE TO BREATHE IS CREATED BY VIRTUE OF ITS NON-EXISTENCE.

The breath originates from this space. This is the vital force or the creative energy of universe, the testimony of the abundant state or the default state of the universal consciousness which is always at play. Similarly, there is gap between subsequent thoughts. Focus your attention and try to widen the gap consciously until the ego mind disappears. Then what is left is only the consciousness which is the creative energy that fulfils your desires and creates a reality based on it. That which we call MANIFESTATION.

By focusing on these spaces, we pull our consciousness back to THE PRESENT MOMENT and it is in this space where the creative energy of the universal consciousness gets connected to our consciousness. This is the time when we have to seed our intention / desires into the universe and watch the magic of the creative energy of the universe to bring them into your physical reality.

BE CAUSE!

Chapter 8- THE KILLER: DISTRUST

NO PHENOMENON, IN THIS UNIVERSE IS EVER SIMPLY REPEATED AGAIN. EVERY SINGLE MOMENT, EVERY SINGLE OCCURRENCE OF THIS UNIVERSE IS UNIQUE

VIII

THE KILLER: DISTRUST

I AM- *By being in the spaces and deeply in the present moment you learn to accept the situation as it is without being judgemental and reactive over it.*

You also get detached from the fear of doubt of your desires being fulfilled or not. Because this connection with the present moment will erase your distrust. You will then operate from abundant creative energy of the universal consciousness.

ME- *What if the thoughts come back and I go back to the distrust phase?*

I AM- *There is no phase. Yes, you heard it. You are what you choose to be. You say I am that, then you are. Starting from that particular moment.*

The reason you go back to the distrust phase is because you start seeking for validation as soon as you say claim to step into your reality. You seek validation in the physical reality.

ME- *But you only said that you become that or have that right in that moment, so automatically I would want to!*

I AM- *Here is the catch;* **the moment you claim your desires/new reality MUST also be the moment of surrender.** *Now, the universe has a way of working and unfolding things or its magic to you in its own way. The way of uncertainty. Every single time universe does something it is unique although to you it might be the similar process or occurrence. To you it might be the Sun but every Sunrise is different.*

No phenomenon, in this universe is ever simply repeated. Every single moment, every single occurrence of this UNIVERSE is unique.

Universe has abundantly infinite ways of doing the same thing which you might believe (by virtue of your ego mind conditioning) could happen only in A CERTAIN WAY possible. You can never know which of these the universe is going to give you.

Therefore, your job is simply to surrender, tell your ego mind to be quite for a while and simply watch the beauty of the universe unfold in the most beautiful and unexpected way.

Chapter 9- EFFORTLESSNESS

A WAY THAT REVEALS ITSELF THE MOST EASILY WHEN WE ARE NOT LOOKING

IX

EFFORTLESSNESS

ME- *Yeah! I get it now. You know how sometimes we say OH! I never imagined that, or I never saw that coming.*

How sometimes very unexpectedly we receive someone's call or get an important email, get money effortlessly or meet people that change our life completely.

I AM- *Exactly! This takes you to your next state- the state of effortlessness.*

ME- *But things have always been hard for me. I have done a lot to get to where I am at this moment. It does not matter if I enjoy being in this position. And that is why it is hard for me to surrender.*

I AM- *Yes! You are absolutely right. It is hard. It will be hard.*

ME- *So, you agree to it? That is all. You have no answer for it?*

Just now I had grown some expectations out of you and here you are shackling them all with a straight face sitting in front of me unmoving.

I AM- *haha! That is it. Amazing !*

You have got it all know. Infact, you knew already. You just have uttered out all that you need to know and proved, we always have that what we need, it's always inside of us.

ME- *What , what are you even talking ?! I am very confused at this point.*

You are saying that I know all I need to know and then also claiming that things are and will be hard for me. Now, that's double standards.

I guess you are again going to give me a shocker, so as you yourself said, I am not going to think much. I just know you are going to give me a way period.

I AM- *haha! That's also true. You are again right.*

Chapter 10- THE ESSENCE OF SURRENDERING

BEST WAY TO LIVE LIFE IS TO LET LIFE LIVE ITSELF

X

THE ESSENCE OF SURRENDERING

I AM- *I am actually pretty impressed that you have started to follow the path to your desires already.*

Let's talk a little bit more about effortlessness.

It is the essence of surrender. Surrendering to life is

Allow life to live itself.

You rush things, you try to micromanage every aspect of it and somehow think you have a control over it or I would say you get this illusion of being the controller which is not coming from your being rather coming from a sense of fear.

Fear of missing out opportunities, fear of losing time and what not. But the truth is life knows how to live, there is nothing you can control about it and that is exactly what makes it magical. Because uncertainty means anything is possible. Your job is simply to trust and watch how universe gives you your desires.

Let its beauty unfold itself before you. When you stop chasing things and do not force life. Universe senses that energy of silence, the energy of calmness, the energy of stillness, THE ENERGY OF SIMPLY BEING. Your desires start to chase you. You will be able to notice and appreciate the ease of universe in working mode. Its effortless, flawless, and magical.

It unfolds in ways that you could never have imagined with ego mind. This is when you will realize how effortless life is. That is the moment surrendering will become easier, it will come naturally to you. You will be free of your anxiety, worry and sense of control and despair.

You will know how to work with universe, talk to it your desires and tell your worries if you have any and let it handle them for you.

The Best way to live life is to let life live itself.

chapter 11- BEING

WE ARE HUMAN BEINGS AND OUR PRIME JOB IS TO JUST BE

XI

BEING

ME- *You are saying that I decide and choose my desires , know that they are true right in this moment. surrender to universe and watch the magic of uncertainty bring my desires into the reality / 3d world which my ego mind understands to be of value. Meanwhile be in a state of abundance; for abundance being the default state, rather than of lack and fear. Let life live itself.*

I am ready to do that all and in fact, I feel closer than ever to my desires. But my question is IF life can live itself and the universe will give you everything you desire by simply choosing your desire to be your reality. That's sounds like a job already done.

I AM- *Yes, you are right, it does mean a job already done!*

ME- *What would I do then? What am I supposed to do here? What would I be doing in here?*

I AM- *You BE. Simply BE. We are human beings. Our prime job is to just BE.*

ME- *Yes, tell me about it.*

I AM- *To BE is to realize your core / fundamental nature. Connecting with the supreme consciousness. Realizing your true nature/ POWER OF BEING YOU. Yes, tell yourself that which you truly are. Claim it.*

I AM THAT!

I am that I am! Yes, that is your true nature.

You are everything that ever existed, existing or would exist.

You are everything that ever happened, happening or would happen.

You are everything you ever desired, desiring or would desire.

You are everything that was loved, is loved and would always be loved.

You are everything that was possible, is possible and could ever be possible.

Realizing I AM THAT is what is BEING.

I AM ONENESS, THE SUPREME CONSCIOUSNESS OR THE UNIVERSE, ABUNDANCE OR THE UNBORN, EXISTING OR NOTHINGNESS, SILENCE OR MELODY, POTENTIAL OR THE ENERGY. I AM GOD. I AM THAT. I AM YOU. I AM BEING.

I AM- Do you still want to be something else? Do you still want do something else? What do you want to run after now? what do you want to chase? Where do you want to be?

ME- Does not speak anything,

(has no words to say, no questions to ask, nowhere to rush) for **I have come to myself.**

My eyes said with words of tears rolling down my cheek screaming joy in every moment of its being.

Chapter 12- THE ARRIVAL

WRITE IT

XII

THE ARRIVAL